WHERE'S THE UNICORN NOW?

ILLUSTRATED BY PAUL MORAN

WRITTEN BY SOPHIE SCHREY

DESIGNED BY JOHN BIGWOOD AND JACK CLUCAS

Michael O'Mara Books Limited

UNICORNS ON TOUR

It's been a busy year for the unicorns of Rainbow Valley. The blessing has become something of an overnight sensation after their first hide-and-seek adventure made the headlines. Due to popular demand, the unicorns are trotting off on a world tour to meet their adoring fans and to spread their magic far and wide.

Can you find all seven unicorns in every scene? They are brilliant at hiding, so you'll have to search high and low!

Find the answers, plus extra things to spot, at the back of the book.

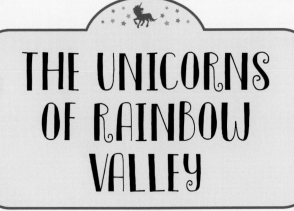

THE UNICORNS OF RAINBOW VALLEY

LEAF

Age: 17 (in unicorn years)

Best-known for: His fearless sense of adventure

Favourite food: Blended-grass smoothie

Motto: Always be where your hooves are

RUBY

Age: 35 (in unicorn years)

Best-known for: Her big heart and top-notch organization skills

Favourite food: Glitter Forest gateau

Motto: Never look a 'gift unicorn' in the mouth

SNOWFLAKE

Age: 41 (in unicorn years)

Best-known for: His sensitive soul and words of advice

Favourite food: Steamed hay

Motto: If you believe, you can achieve

BLOSSOM

Age: 15 (in unicorn years)

Best-known for: Her thick glossy mane and sense of style

Favourite food: Stir-fried leaves

Motto: Be more unicorn, always

LUNA

Age: 21 (in unicorn years)

Best-known for: Winning gold in the Unilympics

Favourite food: Magic mud pie

Motto: Take the unicorn by the horn every day

STARDUST

Age: 9 (in unicorn years)

Best-known for: Always being the first unicorn to crack a joke

Favourite food: Unicorn frappé

Motto: Be a unicorn in a field of horses

AMETHYST

Age: 11 (in unicorn years)

Best-known for: Always having her head buried in a book

Favourite food: Rainbow waffles

Motto: Without the rain, there will be no rainbow

5

FLIGHTS	
LHZ62 Düsseldorf	A11
AB819 Zurich	C4
LDZ60 London	B4
LHZ06 Frankfurt	B1
SN258 Brussels	A4
LH303 Stuttgart	A3
AT403 Athens	C3

BBA

FLIGHTS

LHZ62 Düsseldorf	A11
AB819 Zurich	C4
LDZ60 London	B4
LHZ06 Frankfurt	B1
SN258 Brussels	A4
LH303 Stuttgart	A3
AT403 Athens	C3

JETSETTERS

After a long flight, the unicorns have landed safely at their first destination. It was the blessing's first time in an aeroplane and being up in the clouds was truly magical.

Luna and Blossom are giddy with excitement – they can barely keep their hooves still as they wait for their luggage at baggage reclaim. Stardust is giving interviews to some reporters who have spotted the unicorns in arrivals.

Let the tour begin!

Can you spot all of the unicorns?

VIP TREATMENT

The blessing is whisked from the airport to a swanky hotel for the start of the tour.

When Ruby checks the unicorns in she is delighted to discover that they have been upgraded to the penthouse suite. The views from the room are stunning and the luxury bedding is fluffier than clouds.

While the rest of the family snooze after the long journey, Blossom and Luna head straight to the spa for a full hooficure and some five-star treatment.

Can you spot all of the unicorns?

LONDON, UK

First stop, London – the city that made the unicorns of Rainbow Valley famous and a place they hold very close to their hearts.

In between the busy schedule of interviews and photoshoots, the family finds time to trot out and explore. Blossom has read all about the Royal Family and their ancestors, and to see Buckingham Palace is a dream come true. She's rearing up at the railings, hoping to catch a glimpse of the Queen.

Can you spot all of the unicorns?

ST ANTON, AUSTRIA

The unicorns have a couple of free days in between tour stops, so they decide to try out their skills on the slopes at the picturesque resort of St Anton.

Leaf takes to the snow like a pro and heads off in search of something called a 'black run'. Amethyst is struggling to master the skis, even on the baby slopes, and after falling horn over hoof for the third time, she and Stardust trot off to get a head start on the après-ski activities.

Can you spot all of the unicorns?

VENICE, ITALY

Amethyst is delighted to be visiting Venice. Her favourite novel is set in this fairytale city and she's spent hours back in the Valley daydreaming of floating through the canals in a gondola. *So* romantic.

Some of the unicorns are spotted by a group of tourists in the Piazza San Marco, and Stardust is happy to greet the fans and sign autographs with his horn. Meanwhile, Ruby kicks back with a cappuccino and slice of tiramisu in the sun – bliss.

Can you spot all of the unicorns?

ALL ABOARD

The train has arrived to take the unicorns to their next exciting destination. Snowflake tells Blossom to watch their luggage while he trots off to collect the tickets, and Ruby goes in search of some tasty snacks for the journey.

Luna and Leaf amuse themselves by playing a game of hide-and-seek, and Luna is particularly proud of the hiding spot she has chosen. Will Leaf find her in time to catch their train?

Can you spot all of the unicorns?

Café de Paris

PARIS, FRANCE

It doesn't take long for Luna to fall in love with Paris – the fashion, the food, the romance, the art. It couldn't be a more magical place.

While Blossom and Amethyst are planning which chic boutiques to visit first, Ruby is trying to persuade Stardust to climb the Eiffel Tower with her. He doesn't fancy the queues, and doesn't want to admit that he is scared of heights. He'd far rather while away the hours people watching from a cute café, with an ice-cold drink in hoof.

Can you spot all of the unicorns?

BOULANGERIE

DELPHI, GREECE

It's been a busy few days for the family in Greece, but they've found time to visit the Temple of Apollo. Some of the earliest recordings of unicorns were from ancient Greek writers, and it's a privilege for the blessing to have the opportunity to learn about their ancestors.

Hearing that the unicorns of Rainbow Valley were coming, the locals have staged a special performance in their honour, with impressive costumes and beautiful music. The unicorns can't wait to share some of their own wisdom and magic with the crowd.

Can you spot all of the unicorns?

GIZA, EGYPT

Ruby couldn't let a trip to Egypt pass without a visit to the mighty pyramids. She thinks the Great Sphinx of Giza, with the body of a lion and the head of a man, is the most magnificent statue she's ever seen.

Some of the other unicorns are less impressed. They're melting in the blistering heat and the humidity is giving Blossom's mane a mind of its own. Leaf is getting restless. He's bored of touring endless sights, but Snowflake has promised they'll do something more adventurous on their next stop.

Can you spot all of the unicorns?

WHITEWATER RAFTING

The blessing has signed up for a whitewater rafting adventure. Their guide promises it will be an unforgettable experience, but stresses that they must keep their horns away from the sides of the inflatable rafts. There is a high risk of causing a puncture.

Stardust anticipates it being an experience he'd rather forget. He hates being out of control, and those whirling rapids look SCARY! Meanwhile, daredevil Leaf is in his element – there's no stopping him as he paddles off at top speed down the thundering river.

Can you spot all of the unicorns?

NEW YORK, USA

It's the end of a busy day for the unicorns in the Big Apple, with back-to-back press interviews and photoshoots. They even made a special appearance on a prime-time TV show.

Now it's time to let their manes down and hit the bright lights of Broadway. Luna loves the buzz of the city, with its cool neon signs and high-rise buildings. Leaf makes a beeline for Unicorner, a shop which claims to sell EVERYTHING unicorn related. He spots a poster advertising 'Unicorn World'. What could that be, he wonders?

Can you spot all of the unicorns?

SANTA CRUZ, USA

Stardust can see himself getting used to the laid-back, sunny Californian vibes. Everyone is so chilled out and friendly. He's already been offered a free surfing lesson while he was picking up a green juice at the beach café.

Ruby is ready to plunge horn-first into the sea, and Snowflake is busy trotting up and down the boardwalk, admiring the glorious vintage funfair. The sweet smell of candy floss reminds him of being back in Rainbow Valley.

Can you spot all of the unicorns?

RIO DE JANEIRO, BRAZIL

Carnival is in full swing when the blessing lands in Rio de Janeiro, and the unicorns are ready to PARTY! The streets are alive with people dancing, spectacular colours, jubilant music and incredible costumes. Amethyst has never seen so much glitter and sparkle – and that's unusual for a unicorn.

Leaf and Stardust are trying to master samba dancing, but they keep tripping over their hooves. Everyone makes it look so easy, but moving their hips and legs to the rhythm of the drums is not coming naturally to the unicorns.

Can you spot all of the unicorns?

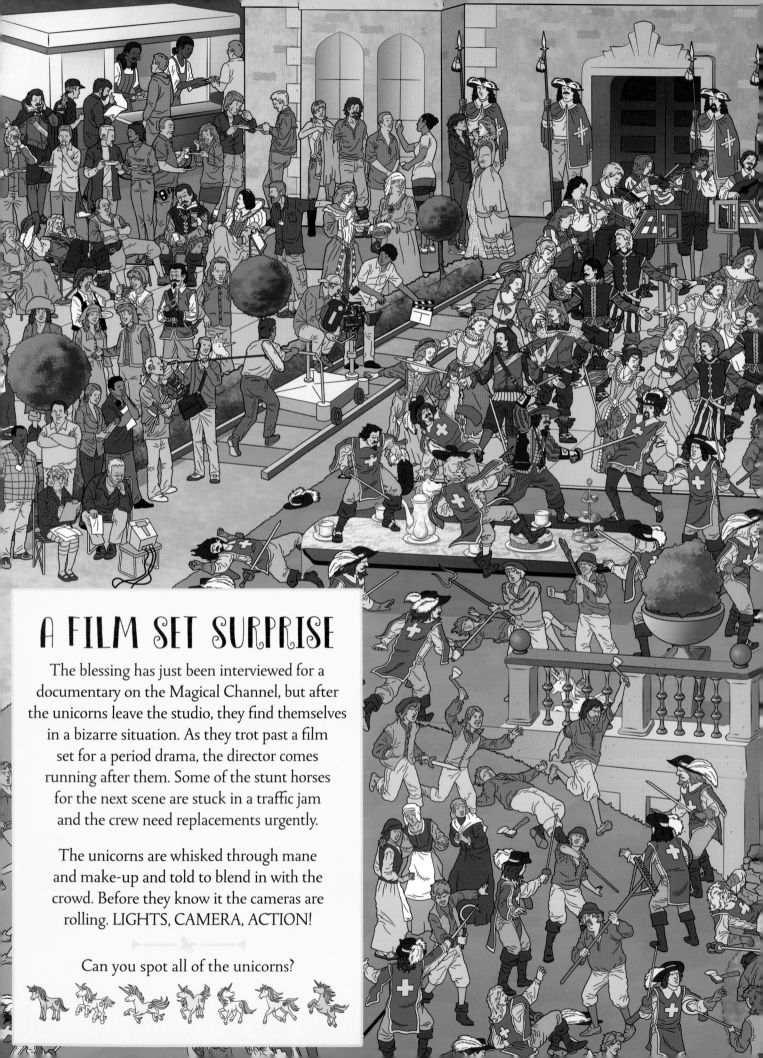

A FILM SET SURPRISE

The blessing has just been interviewed for a documentary on the Magical Channel, but after the unicorns leave the studio, they find themselves in a bizarre situation. As they trot past a film set for a period drama, the director comes running after them. Some of the stunt horses for the next scene are stuck in a traffic jam and the crew need replacements urgently.

The unicorns are whisked through mane and make-up and told to blend in with the crowd. Before they know it the cameras are rolling. LIGHTS, CAMERA, ACTION!

Can you spot all of the unicorns?

UNDER THE SEA

After much persuasion from Leaf, all seven
unicorns have taken the plunge and gone
diving on the Great Barrier Reef in Australia.
Luna is especially anxious, but Leaf reassures
her that her horn will act as a snorkle.

Ruby is enjoying the tranquility and silence
of being under the sea – it's like another world.
Amethyst is transfixed by the rainbow-coloured
fish and beautiful coral, while Stardust is trying
to track down something called a narwhal –
the unicorn of the sea, apparently.

Can you spot all of the unicorns?

DINOSAUR FUN

It's the blessing's last day in Australia and Ruby has organized a trip to a dinosaur museum. The exhibit promises to transport visitors back to the prehistoric world, but the whole experience is a bit too realistic for poor Blossom. The unicorns are surrounded by giant, moving dinosaurs and she's terrified!

Luna isn't phased by the mighty beasts and Stardust has got horn envy. Did the *Triceratops* really need three horns? It's rather showy, in his opinion.

Can you spot all of the unicorns?

UNICORN WORLD

The family are coming to the end of their trip, but there's a final surprise in store. They've been invited to officially open 'Unicorn World', a magical place dedicated to the unicorns of Rainbow Valley, created by the Horse Collective – the unicorns' ultimate super-fan club.

The blessing is overwhelmed by the number of horses who've turned out to welcome them. It's a special moment as the sun begins to set behind the glistening rainbow. The tour has been an incredible experience and the memories will stay with the unicorns forever.

Can you spot all of the unicorns?

ANSWERS

SPOTTER'S CHECKLIST

A monkey-shaped package

A man with a mop

A woman holding pink flowers

A man proposing to his girlfriend

Two plane spotters

A child wearing a red cap

A girl with a big teddy bear

Three 'no entry' signs

Two purple suitcases

A woman eating an apple

JETSETTERS

VIP TREATMENT

SPOTTER'S CHECKLIST

Someone building a house of cards

A man on a tiny bike

A man with a guitar case

A child drawing on hotel property

A woman doing the vacuuming

Someone yelling at the hotel manager

Someone riding on a hotel trolley

A waiter with a bottle of champagne

A man playing the violin

A child standing on a chair

LONDON, UK

SPOTTER'S CHECKLIST

A news reporter ☐

A blue trumpet ☐

A lost camera ☐

A guard in the wrong trousers ☐

A man hugging his daughter ☐

A girl sucking her thumb ☐

Two Union Jack flags ☐

A sunburnt man ☐

Some stripy trousers ☐

A purple rucksack ☐

SPOTTER'S CHECKLIST

Cups of coffee being spilt ☐

A man eating a bag of doughnuts ☐

Two alpine rescue doctors ☐

A red and yellow snowboard ☐

A man with a red bow tie ☐

Someone relaxing on the ski lift ☐

Some dangerous driving ☐

A child learning to ski ☐

A snowboarder with a goatee beard ☐

A man getting his hat knocked off ☐

ST ANTON, AUSTRIA

VENICE, ITALY

SPOTTER'S CHECKLIST

A monk ☐

A man with mismatched shoes ☐

A polka-dot costume ☐

A violinist ☐

A polka-dot tie ☐

One yellow glove ☐

Four couples holding hands ☐

Two gold masks ☐

A girl in purple waiting for her date ☐

A waitress on her way home ☐

ALL ABOARD

SPOTTER'S CHECKLIST

A man falling over on the stairs ☐

A woman carrying a stack of presents ☐

A couple arguing ☐

A girl with pink hair ☐

A boy playing with a toy train ☐

Two people eating ice cream ☐

A man on a bike ☐

A guard with a flag ☐

Two people sliding down the banisters ☐

Someone carrying a skateboard ☐

SPOTTER'S CHECKLIST

A birthday cake ☐

A cat among the pigeons ☐

A man with a walking stick ☐

A man on a laptop ☐

A saxophone player ☐

A woman eating crisps ☐

A man with a purple briefcase ☐

Lost boys with a map ☐

A woman with pink sunglasses ☐

A man sweeping ☐

PARIS, FRANCE

BOULANGERIE

Café de Paris

DELPHI, GREECE

SPOTTER'S CHECKLIST

The Pythia, the priestess of the oracle ☐

Two people meditating ☐

A man with wings on his helmet ☐

A woman on a man's shoulders ☐

A woman reading a scroll ☐

A man with a trident ☐

A man waving ☐

Thirteen goats ☐

A man tripping up ☐

A soldier whose helmet is on fire ☐

GIZA, EGYPT

WHITEWATER RAFTING

NEW YORK, USA

SANTA CRUZ, USA

SPOTTER'S CHECKLIST

A yellow kite

A bodybuilder

A human pyramid

A stray dog

A man with a frisbee

A boy with turtle armbands

A football

Someone who can't swim

A guitar-jamming session

A man carrying green shoes

SPOTTER'S CHECKLIST

A man in a green wig

Sixteen blue balloons

A woman with a purple handbag

A drummer

An orange baseball cap

Some tasselled trousers

A polka-dot bikini

White elbow gloves

An orange bag

A dancer with mismatched shoes

RIO DE JANEIRO, BRAZIL

A FILM SET SURPRISE

SPOTTER'S CHECKLIST

Someone playing a harp

Some sandwiches

A woman with lilac hair

A man with a loudspeaker

Someone wearing a red scarf

A musketeer on the phone

Someone holding a basket

Two actors having make-up done

A man falling down the stairs

A teapot

UNDER THE SEA

SPOTTER'S CHECKLIST

A pink lobster ☐

Two fish with big pink lips ☐

An ugly eel ☐

A jellyfish ☐

A swordfish ☐

A dawdling clown fish ☐

A red crab ☐

Seven fish with a diamond pattern ☐

Two turtles ☐

A pair of yellow flippers ☐

SPOTTER'S CHECKLIST

A dino with a bright mohican ☐

A dino relaxing on its back ☐

Five dragonflies ☐

A tiny dino climbing high ☐

A dino trampling on another's head ☐

Three flying dinosaurs ☐

A *Stegosaurus* ☐

A *Triceratops* ☐

An *Allosaurus* ☐

Four green dinos wading in the water ☐

DINOSAUR FUN

UNICORN WORLD

SPOTTER'S CHECKLIST

A superhero horse ☐

A human shoe ☐

Two snorkelling horses ☐

Three pink satchels ☐

A wizard horse ☐

A kite ☐

Two golden horseshoes ☐

A unicorn onesie ☐

A foal being carried ☐

A ballerina horse ☐

Published in Great Britain in 2018 by Michael O'Mara Books Limited,
9 Lion Yard, Tremadoc Road, London SW4 7NQ

W www.mombooks.com

f Michael O'Mara Books

y @OMaraBooks

Additional artwork by Stuart Taylor, Wan (Big Red Illustration) and Steve Wiltshire

A CIP catalogue record for this book is available from the British Library.

ISBN: 978-1-78929-061-5

1 3 5 7 9 10 8 6 4 2

This book was printed in August 2018 by L.E.G.O.,
Viale dell'Industria 2, 36100, Vicenza, Italy.